for my grandmothers

in memory

Connie Renton Macfarlane

and

Alice Fitzgerald Fellows

The Powerlines

Gerrie Fellows

Polygon

Polygon
An imprint of Edinburgh University Press Ltd
22 George Square, Edinburgh

Typeset in Bembo by
Hewer Text Ltd, Edinburgh, and
printed and bound in Great Britain by
Bell & Bain Ltd, Glasgow

A CIP record for this book is
available from the British Library

ISBN 0 7486 6278 2 (paperback)

The Publisher acknowledges subsidy from

THE SCOTTISH ARTS COUNCIL

towards the publication of this volume.

The tests I need to pass are prescribed by the spirits
of place   who understand travel but not amnesia
(Adrienne Rich, 'The Spirit of Place')

CONTENTS

ACKNOWLEDGEMENTS

Thanks are due to many people and institutions for help in the writing of *The Powerlines*: first, to the Scottish Arts Council for the award of a Travel and Research Grant and to Air New Zealand; also to the Scottish Arts Council and Renfrew District Libraries for the Writing Fellowship which I held at Paisley Central Library during 1993–95; to staff of the Hocken and Turnbull libraries and the Canterbury Museum in New Zealand, and of the Mitchell and Edinburgh University Libraries and the Eyemouth Museum in Scotland; to Cath Brown, Jonathan Mane and Bob Offer, who were kind enough to spend time answering my rather vague questions, though none of them is responsible for what I have made of our conversations, anymore than are the friends and family who welcomed me as a guest, drove me around, made introductions, told family stories or were simply themselves – New Zealanders; thanks go to them all, in particular to my uncle Les Fellows, who died before *The Powerlines* was published, and to Donna Goodliffe, Ray Burrell, Jane Donaldson and John Boyle and Cameron, Claire Backes and Keith, Paul and Pippy Macfarlane. Love and thanks go especially to Dugald and Fran Macfarlane who helped me to connect my past with my present and whose book this has in part become; to my parents, Al and Geraldine Fellows, for remembering; to Maggie for our sibling life; and to Tom, who has shared this book's slow gestation with me.

Many thanks go also to Tom Leonard, Gerry Loose, Alan Riach and especially to Robyn Marsack for taking the time to read and comment on *The Powerlines* in its various incarnations.

Acknowledgements are due to the journals in which some of

these poems and prose pieces were first published: *The Cambridge Journal of Contemporary Criticism, Chapman, Cutting Teeth,* the *Edinburgh Review, New Writing Scotland, Southfields Review* and to BBC Radio Scotland.

Acknowledgement is made also to The Hakluyt Society for permission to quote from *The Journals of Captain James Cook,* edited by J. C. Beaglehole and to Adrienne Rich and W. W. Norton & Co. Inc for permission to quote from 'The Spirit of Place' from *A Wild Patience has Taken Me This Far, Poems 1978–1981* by Adrienne Rich.

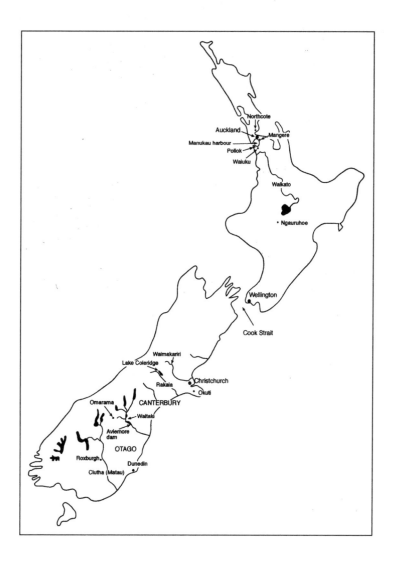

Northcote
Auckland
Mangere
Manukau harbour
Pollok
Waiuku
Waikato
• Ngauruhoe
Wellington
Cook Strait
Waimakariri
Lake Coleridge
Rakaia
Christchurch
• Okuti
Omarama
CANTERBURY
Waitaki
Aviemore
dam
OTAGO
Roxburgh.
Dunedin
Clutha (Matau)

A Chronicle of Beginnings

I

Deptford   I imagine them leaving
London Scots, pulling their roots up
through half a generation of thin soil

Arms akimbo over the crates
of fine wine   the drawing-room carpet
the pianoforte
The women packing the linen   the family
silver   the signed copies
of Dickens   The feudal insignia
wrapped in embroidered samplers   cushion
covers   the sewing silks in their books
of notched card   pages of pure gold

> *On 4th September 1850*
> *from Gravesend*
> *for New Zealand*
> *on the Sir George Seymour*
> *Chief cabin   List no. 20*

They set forth on the wastes of ocean
with only God and the Empire to bring them comfort
The seas tossed sheet music   written language
Iron bands tightened around casks of sour water
The ship rocked with its cargo of hope
with bricks and slates and casement sashes
with sicknesses and births
with slop pails and bed pans and ship's closets
with smells and blood
with sheep slaughtered beside the long boat
with dead children   tiny bodies swung into the deep
The Lord be praised, only infants have been taken
with coffee and lime-juice   pearl-barley
with cooking pots swung in steerage
with the memory of dances under the lustrous stars
with dreams and futures
with love
and the ferocious certainty of rightness

II

In the beginning   was absence
without mass   void
tenuous with potential
seeded with future
visionary   fabulous   fictive
broody with night

From the plane   a vapour trail
the Pacific below us a dark basin of winter ocean
seeded with mist

A myriad breath over the body of ocean
gave birth to the Sky
Sky and Earth lay clasped together
a form   a canoe prow
carved over corrugations of water
Ranginui   Papatuanuku
and between them Tane Mahuta
a rooted trunk flung heavenwards
bore up Sky from Earth
so that light might filter into the world

A form   uprising.   We are flying to meet it
the plane coasting in darkness   the wing tip
touched with light   One by one the stars
and beneath us mantled in night
the coral-fretted seaweed-emblazoned ocean
from which Maui with the jawbone of his grandmother
fished up the island   as I fish my native land
dark wing of birth   out of the sea of memory and origin
imagining   the peopled earth

III

A canoe prow riding the throat of a whirlpool
spirals turned skeletal by wind and water
foam-carved stories of voyage and landfall

How the navigators came with seeds and plantings
How they brought kumara   dog   rat
the pattern of a braided net   a skein
of sound with which they named the islands   each
indentation of coast   each landform
How they traced the veins of the foliage
the sinew of the country   How they paced
the islands   How they made them home
a place of human habitation
a lace of stories   artifice
and artifact   warfare   ritual   love

How they told of those who had glided here
over coruscations of water
those who had travelled on airy lumps of pumice
those who had floated on calabashes

of Kupe who cut up the islands
of Tamatea who travelled through the land
of Rakaihaitu who dug out the waterpools
of those who had gone ahead and called forth fire
or set stone mauri in the forests
of those who were turned to mountains
or to weeping   or to pillars of rock
how the fish became greenstone
and the rock that was light
became heavy with tapu
how the sacred canoes became the country

These things became the land. The land became them

A grooved stone anchor dropped into deep ocean
and that anchor was blood   history   language
umbilicus

IV

A word   written
in a ripple of ink on sand where blood was spilt
a fingerprint on the map of rumour through which
an English mariner conjured his ship
real and small as a nut
towards empirical fact: soil   beach
a hilly surface cloathed with Verdure

These were his entries:
This was chart   measurement   record:
time and the sun's angle
tide   wind force   the sounding of ocean
estuary, elevation, anchorage
the empirical fact of others
dayly we saw smookes

This was the measurement
of the body   of earth   of the human
body   of water   of bone
shell, feather, fish scale   *the sand banks*
well store'd with Cockles, and clams
and in many places were Rock Oysters

This was the record
of grasses, groves of timber   iron sand
of *soil rich and proper for cultivation*
of *a brave, open, warlike people*
their skins, nets, gestures, gardens
gods, grammar, voices, weapons

This was the map
of a country: *Two large Islands divided*
by a strait or passage of 4 or 5 Leagues broad

fixed in the chart of the English language

V

Welcome to New Zealand

Please help us to protect New Zealand agriculture and forestry industries from overseas pests and diseases by answering all these questions

Do you have with you:

animals (alive or dead)   myself, the dead cells my skin sloughs off, my living blood and breath, **animal products including meat**   my own flesh, the network of my nerves, my lungs in the basket of my ribs, **skins**   these layers of tissue and the dipped beds of follicles, fingerprints, **feathers**   the delicate, waving fingers of the ileum, **bone**   this skeleton, calcium laden from a milky country, **wool**   my nest of pubic hair, **eggs**   the ova I carry in their curled fern fronds, **cultures**   two, **shells**   my ears, the rosy receptacles of language, **hair**   these streaked colours entwined, dark for the north, gold for the south, **honey**   the milk of my vagina, my mouth's saliva:
This is a map of myself

plants   from the compost of the dead, **fruit, vegetables**   fibrous text, narrative thread, **seed**   unwritten, **flowers**   blossom of speech, **nuts, bulbs**   hard kernals of waiting, **straw**   mulch of paper and tussock, **bamboo**   at the border of a garden a bow scraping, **wood, plant products**   growth, and a parable of the sugars:
This is a record   a transformation

equipment used with animals; things to treat or prevent pests or disease in animals   antibody, mnemonic of inoculation:
This is memory   This is the body's information

used tents and other camping equipment; used sporting equipment; soil   groundwork of atom and worm cast:
This is the map of a country

In the last 30 days have you:
visited a farm, forest, abattoir or meat-packing place?
These are the entries, in the beginning   birth and death:
This is the map of a journey.

I

Bloodlines

The Storybook Pages

> Chief cabin   List No. 20
> Mr D. Macfarlane
> Mrs D. Macfarlane
> Marion   aged 15
> Dugald   aged 12
> Kate   aged 7
> Norman   aged 6
> Alice   aged 3
> Flora   infant

How often we were told   how they came

as if they were the first   as if the histories

were one history   as if it were linear

a simple line of ascent

The story of it   when we were children

watching them arrive   in procession

Dugald Macfarlane among the patriarchs
the high Anglicans
The ladies in crinolines   (Mary Ann his wife
their good Scotch maid)
always   absurdly with hatboxes   struggling
towards a future of picket fences and geraniums
And we   their great great grandchildren
the fifth generation here in this country
gazing at them   as if they were the first

as if the world had begun here   before Christ's College

the Anglican Cathedral   the Heathcote Tunnel
as if they'd come over the bridle path
the mountains blotted out in January haze
and halted there   and said

This country is a blank page on which we will write our names
Even its geology is ours to label

*From the crater of Ngauruhoe the guardian of the sacred fires
sent flame to Tamatea the great traveller*

They entered like children among the lavas

They did not know this

They thought they were conquerers.

> ON THIS SPOT THE PIONEER
> WOMEN OF CANTERBURY
> AND THEIR FAMILIES
> RESTED AFTER THE CLIMB
> FROM THE PORT OF LYTTELTON
> AND GAZED WITH AWE BUT
> WITH COURAGE UPON THE
> HILLS AND PLAINS OF
> CANTERBURY WHERE THEY
> WERE TO MAKE THEIR HOMES

They might have imagined smoke
in the scent of scrub from the plain
voices in the breeze which rippled along the summits

They paused in his footprints   and said

This country is a blank page   Here we will write our names.

A nor-wester surges through the portholes of the shelter
its stones scored with other names and dates   other arrivals:

14

MAFUTAGA, M
VAILOA. PALAULI
SAVAII.
WESTERN SAMOA.
15/12/1986

AFA. M
POLYNESIAN AIRLINE
WESTERN SAMOA.
15/8/87

RAMATA M
SOCIAL WELFARE

Canterbury Museum Negative No. 1285:
Dugald Macfarlane

My gravestone a blank   my name an absence
yet my name continues   a glossed museum monochrome

Out of the tone and grain history makes of me
I protest   I was verb and colour   one
of the makers of history in whose wake the marsh
thrives with buildings, pavements where pukekos stalked
South to the Waitaki we stocked the plain with sheep
Across the Rakaia were verandahed mansions
In town we made money, the laws of the province

You read your own splittings into my cameo of silence
shifting plates of rock and time will not let me be
a warrior with a right to stories, sword
embroidered in my dexter hand   proud of the buckle
from the shoe I wore to rout Napoleon, the medal
on my coat's frayed husk   thrilling to embarkation
each setting out   to battle or another life

To my sons (for we have always been fighting men)
I passed the buckle and our blood's emblazoned scroll
Shaded with willows from Bonaparte's tomb, I set forth
for God and Empire   a demi savage
born again into a skirl of pipes and tartan

Mary Ann Macfarlane:
A Shopping List & Notes towards a Complaint

Am I to be given no recognition   who learned
to live out the hot nor-westerly blusters of November
and the cloud of my husband's discontent?

12″ green silk ribbon
½lb of Muscat raisins

For years our meat was barrel beef, salted pork
served from the best china
my piano a sounding board of wind and water
my drawing-room carpet an island in an ocean of tussock

cinnamon
fine bread flour

Beyond the capricious river which ruled our boundaries
the country was a bell tolling the rumour of distance
My sons were at ease in it
I was tossed daily on a voyage of parting

When we lost the sheep with scab
I knew I would not go Home   this was our landfall

mutton fat
caustic soda for soap

Under the new brick house
the wine cellars bloomed with Muscadet and tawny port
My husband told tall stories over the claret
and hoped the colony would bring him fortune

My sons managed the sheep runs of other men

Young Dugald with Dreamscape

In this country I woke to a frosted blanket
a good river horse treading the shallows
the sour smell of sheep in the tussock

From thicket and flax clump, dust cloud:
a river boundary   thousands of acres
of sweet feed; fescue, white clover
the sheep with their heads to the wind

My palms cupped pools of trout ova fringed
by fingers of willow   haybeds, this pasture
4,000 acres to be broken up for cropping
these thousands of acres sown in wheat

I sleep to rumours of moa   polished flints
the plough broken on twisted root
bush by the creeks, dark as memory   fern
a parching and violent wind

The native flora cries its way back in dream

Kate's Song: An Epitaph

Idiot child   No one recalls me
No one notes my death   my life
has been erased from the history books
I have no place   more than a name

This is my story   I was born laughing
I have become silence   This is my story
I was not fit to people this country
I was not a flower   not a thistle
not an English rose

I was an idiot child   I crossed the globe
unperturbed   wondrous, wondering at water
at new smells   at the cruelty of others

I was an idiot child   No one recalls me

Ghost Page for Mary Ann at Racecourse Hill

Gorse   river shingle   scrub   and in clear light
the Waimakariri stirring its argentine channels

It was to have been a window opening on to another country
(outcrops bristling above a farmyard
bracken aflame with spores   the loch rippling)

Was Ledard the name my husband brought from Scotland
or was it the place he named   dun-coloured
cracking with whips of speargrass   wind-strewn
   unbounded?
The name soaked up the silence of the place
the place remained   Changed

Oh wing of river I feared   combed water quietness
I could have loved this tamed country
windbreak   crop pattern   the endless rows

Is this Ledard
these silk green grasses
the straight roads with their delicate nets of shadow?

Ledard is a name without a place
like a spindly wraith between the poplars
a ghostly page in a family almanac

The Stone Pages

In the cemetery beside the Avon
an inscription erased by time and weather
to a blank of sandstone
another faintly legible
the third a chiselled name
All the slabs broken, pitched forwards.

Dugald Macfarlane lies in the swampy soil
of the deceptive plain   anonymous beside his sons.
And the women   Mary Ann Shaw   Anna Young
    from Belfast
are they buried here   having outlived their husbands?
The stones maintain a silence
For this is male ground
The burial place of the forefathers
those who transmitted the lines of heritage
the lines of power.

Does the coloniser in death have a more honourable claim
to the land he usurped?

The head of my ancestor has never been placed in a museum
    display case.
The burying place of his bones is not a municipal golf course.
His gravestone has not been overturned by bulldozers
or mined for ironsands.
Though the solidities are broken,
the gravestones snapped in the night and overturned
their granular surfaces as blank with erased inscription
as the face of the land
my forebears are planted here
among their achievements and their despoilations
a part of the country they changed irrevocably
with their grass and sheep, their monoculture.

Do the dead make the ground sacred?
Are they what roots us?

It is we the living who carry the notches incised in the bone
who carry the past in our faces, our ways of speech and being
our bodies' intractabilities and negations
the gifts and burdens of inheritance

I name the names
I count them back: genial exploiters
and small cogs of empire, men and women of their times

I count them back:
the bloodline, the racial story, the fingerprints of my people
Imagining in them the likenesses of the living
I give them origins and blame.

Narrative Subjects

Interlude   Southern England from 1963

Catching a train west from Waterloo past gravel pits and English history at Runymede, through the coppices of Surrey, arriving (the same every time), turning the corner, Maggie and I running the last bit of the road.

Those who were alive then, Home Renton, his wife Mildred, were my mother's mother's people, still living among the portraits moveable as money, taking winter cruises on the invested proceeds of a small part of Berwickshire. Home in his gardening clothes ambling down to the Conservative club or walking the dogs; Mildred, even years later in her mid-eighties, astonishing small children with her cigarette holder and blood-red nails.

As visiting New Zealanders and then year by year Maggie and I growing up English, we took tea here among the portraits. My father, occupied among his in-laws in copying out the family tree, caught sight of his own name in small black letters in the lower right-hand corner, *married Alwyn Graham Fellows, 14 February 1950.*

Over the years I learnt them face by face: that still British family, drawn out of Scotland; the women haunting and individual, the white-stocked, dark-coated men.

The Heritor

You ask who I am

In my black coat I have become at last as anonymous as those
who were my servants   One among numberless faces
You know me only as a heritor   an owner of property
but not as a man who threw off his frock coat and played tig
with the children

Untruth.   I will never be as anonymous as the fishing folk
or the joiner at the crossroads
You would find me if you tried   My name is everywhere
inscribed on wills and sasines
The houses I lived in were stone built   and have survived
Long after I am gone a street in the town will bear my name
You would find me sure enough among the graded lists of
lawyers and lieutenant colonels   the doctors of medicine
You know who I am

gracing the stairwell   shoulder to black shoulder   repeated
    in oils
imperceptibly changing   whiskered or clean shaven   only
    the cut
of my coat   the ruched style of my cravat alter

Yes,
though I once flung off my frock coat and played tig with the
    children
I am the heritor   the owner of property

An Aureole for a Great Great Grandmother: Frances Wallace Renton (1799–1845)

Is this what I've become   a painted beauty
pensive, far too perfect   emerging from a shadowy alcove
in dark velvet   a pink rose?

My husband's town was honeycombed by rumour, looped
with secrets   the old trade had left its imprint
in a habit of distrust   Walls opened
without signal   I sensed the network of hollows
the multiple irises of the mirrored streets
Shopkeepers smiled and turned their heads away
Nothing was spoken aloud

I turned inward to the sanctuary of the garden
cradled my son at its centre   swung with him
among the patterned leaves of quince and medlar
under the trellis in a sunlit alcove
The petals of the tea rose folded over and over

But no wall can keep out the osmosis of whispers
like convolvulus it twined around the stems
of the espaliers, took root under the flagged paths

There were things I knew which no one spoke of

My child walked proud over the void of the future
its waters lapped him   In them
the waxen faces of the drowned were our own faces
without sound   white flowers in the dark earth

I dreamt there was no time left

Great Grandfather Renton above the Decanters

It will end with me   My children will go out of the country
I will be the last

I will end as an oil painting of a stern and kindly patriarch
David Renton,   Lt Col M.D. 15th Hussars
above the decanters in an English dining room
or beyond the Cape in a country I have never seen

After my death   my wife will go back to her English roots
There will be a war   my younger son's name left in this town
inscribed on stone   but Home   my first born, my
    inheritor
will break the link   will cut his ties with this country
and go south   (Did he hate me so   this fishridden town
this country's dour capital with its skivie winds?)

I married Maria Padbury for her perfect vowels
I sent my sons to an English school
that their speech might be the speech of those who rule
He will go south   His mother's language has taken him

And my daughters: Helen   Frances   Connie
will flee across the oceans to the edges of the Empire
to Africa and the antipodes

It ends here.

Beyond me are photographs

of my unknown granddaughters holding their ponies' mouths
steady before a background of giant flax

Afterthought

You hardly noticed me   hidden
upstairs in the spare bedroom   with your cousin's face

Helen Maria Padbury   known as Minnie   wife of David

You thought me English for my accent and my father's name
but I was Australian   When my husband brought me to
   Eyemouth
the servants (imagine it) were expecting a black woman

I did not dislike the country   I bore my children there:
Home Frank Helen Frances and Connie (darling Didi)
I smiled indulgently as they bred white mice and sold
them at a profit to the locals or the boys, sauntering home
after an afternoon shoot held up the Eyemouth train

But after my husband died   I fled
not as far south as the golden continent of my childhood
but south at least to the warmer climes of convivial Weybridge

Postscript

> The paintings divided up like family plots
> but the field above the sea remains intact
> (It is another's field now   to work
> in the twenty-first century)

They are Dead
There is No One to Speak

I am cast over this wide landscape
tumbling down a wheatfield to the coast

My grandmother would not return

The farmer ploughs his good field
the tractor moving across a sloping rim
the windows of Chesterbank
flare blank gold

They are dead
A stranger has taken the faces from the stair

And I have never belonged
in the line of the lairds

Sitting here at my desk
the hottest day of summer
the reek of sewage from across the river
the dry leaves of your family tree
rustling in my ears

The women losing their names
appear as branches
grafted on
to bear fruit

On the war memorial
Frank's name among the
fathers   brothers   husbands
fallen from the solid troughs
wave after wave

They came from here
The place did not belong to them

They belonged to it
Enough to have their names carved into its heart

My grandmother grew up with the slap of this water
the fishing boats putting out and returning
the stink of fish
the terrible northern sea
Behind the bustle of the harbour
the plain houses facing the north-east salt wind

She put her face to the window pane
She broke ice in her basin

She was – after all – Scottish

Unrooted Poem   Floating
for Connie & Helen & Frances

Of being sisters

Ice cracked across

what exists Of
Black and white fragments
tonal shards
elliptical
un-statements
severings   almosts

framed
static   past

wired together
in the patchy network
of love

Ice cracked across
glaze
of photographs
split
to fleshy
muscle pump
the sodden
embroideries
of the body
Colour

Blood
story

The Notation of a Dream Recounted
by Connie Renton to her Granddaughters

I dreamt the garden was an island rocked in a shoal of tides
its cliff edges   a lighthouse   swayed
A hare ran through the streets
The town disappeared in the sea mist   white air   white waves
broke on the Hurkurs

Spray on the windscreen   the fisherlassies lean on the cars

I dreamt the garden was an island rocked in a shoal of tides
the silver-fletted herrings, the great oaks shaking their curly boughs
A dream of black white silver   a dream of water
the Radiant   the Harmony   the Blossom   the Sweet Home
The house flew in the wind

The fisherlassies lean on the cars and smoke
there is salt on their lips

I dreamt the garden was an island drowned in a wave of stone
its flowers a delicate flotsam flung from the mouth of ocean
the waterlogged bladders of lungs a bloated tideline
the James and Robert   the Janet   the Press Home
broken against the beach of the garden

Through a briny patina we scowl to take
oddly angled photographs   vision stopped wide open in the
    haar

a girl in a phonebox, coat dark in a lantern of luminous panes
a car spun off the road, back windscreen out, lone passenger
    waiting
in whiteness   and the twilight closing

And I didn't know if what I dreamt
was the sound of the gulls   or of the fishergirls calling
the Enterprise   the Invincible   the Forget me Not   the Wave

Photograph of my Grandparents
(A Wartime Romance)

England. An oval of leafy sepia scribble
an ideogram of rural idyll   even in Weybridge
even in wartime

Keith Macfarlane, a New Zealand soldier   Connie Renton
a girl in uniform, have paused   bicycles askew
against that sunlit aura

The photograph is a charmed circle
beyond it lie the churned and broken fields of Flanders
Gallipoli's reef of ANZAC bone

It is she, the ambulance driver   who has transported him
(After the desert war, light without mercy   he feels
TB's scorching fire a kind of balm)

Is he serious or quizzical under his brimmed hat?
In fact, he would like to crack a joke   Poms
are so solemn   part of his convalescence is a mission
to upset the occasion   to make them laugh

Connie smiles
seeing him   she imagines a country without loss
a way of mending the families broken by death

They are drawn into love's charmed circle   their pain
lies beyond it, fading   like the sepia's rosy margin

This is a wartime romance   he is
her handsome soldier   she is his Scottish lass

Tableau

Interlude 1920

Between the old life and the new, on the liner's washed decks, wrapping the tartan rug around her knees, she mourned her darlings: her father, her brother Frank buried in the trench of her heart, her mother whose life had been riven into shrapnel over France, Helen's child (shame buried in silence, not to be spoken of). There on the ocean her heart did not break. It became the cracked vessel containing all this. In it she buried the past, buried Eyemouth, Edinburgh, Weybridge. Turned her face to the new life.

Tableau

The walled garden of her childhood

became   in another country
open   undulant ground
a place of hollows and hill slopes

(How many ways there are to slip through it
as gently as a ghost from childhood
revisiting paradise)

From its beginnings in flame and sawmill
the farm edged back the wild
The orchard was planted with apple trees
pear   French walnut   the vegetable garden
set with rows of potatoes
pumpkins   the silvery stems of beet
In the washhouse among the baskets
and the bulbs stored for autumn
an old Manx cat gave birth
to a lineage of stub-tailed kittens
Okuti had become a familiar map
of paddocks   kennels   woolshed

In the garden my grandmother began
to create a living geometry
of daffodil silk at the edge of the orchard
mauve anemones and the multiple heads
of the polyanthus
waxy shining platefuls of azalea
velvety nemesias, long spike-leaved ixias
African marigolds the colour of egg yolk
nasturtiums twined crisscross over gravel
the blue hydrangea

The calendar of plantings
became swathes of colour, scent, texture
As elaborate as etiquette the garden stirred and bowed
each beautiful head to another

the massed glories of the floral dance

She held the bush at bay   without fences
with the delicate acquisitions of empire

The garden was a pattern and a ritual
a way of approaching perfection

Into it she sank anger loss shame
her own pain and the pain of the letters which came:
Frances miscarrying while her husband drank
and Helen in Africa
what was told between the lines of her letters
what her life was
could not be spoken of   She buried the grief of it
Only her brother was happy
playing the stock market and letting his fine mind
run to seed in Sunningdale

Was she   the youngest, her father's darling
the only one to have learned his dictum
that work makes us
that without it we are nothing?
Her siblings fought him   They thrilled to occasions
her sister-in-law making an entrance
in furs and diamonds
But this was what she wanted   to live in her body
simply   in the open air

It was true
she never quite got used to the country
its lack of deference, the informality   the accent
But she did not want to go back
She bit her lip   and clipped the heads of the roses.

And years later
from the carved desk in Bay View Road   refusing
to visit us in England   she did not write
it's more than forty years, it's another country
but   the garden would go to ruin.

*   *   *

On the visitors' gate my grandfather carved the name Arrochar

As he sauntered down the slope of the lawn at dusk   (the day
    lily
blooming and closing itself up)   the wooden gate opened

to a mythical territory: something ancestral he kept in his name
a motto above a compartment wavy
Not a place   a heraldic field.   Not the incised leaf of the
    oak
or the feathered leaf of the matai   but a shape
as formal as a playing card   a spade on a cloth of tartan

Nothing real   Nothing we needed now.

*   *   *

My grandmother woke in the night
hearing my mother's sleeping feet glide
out of the french doors of the bedroom   across the verandah
crunching the milky quartz pebbles of the path
silently crossing the dewy lawn

a morepork shrilling   the stalks of the bamboo
shifting and scraping at the feathery brim of the bush
its greeny shade calling

There is a way of moving
out of the hem of the moonlight into the bush
footfalls almost quiet   you pause   your eyes

grown used to the dark
There is a way
of stepping out from the heraldic flora of empire
and stepping into leaf vein   deep pools of water over stone

Listen

The people of the place are here before us

There is a way of passing through the bush
of coming to stand at the edge of the lawn at night
observing the cut borders   the heraldic flora of empire

There are other voices

There is a way of listening

*   *   *

A footstep on a track down a hill slope at dusk   (the day
    closing
crumples itself up)   The gate opens

to smoke blowing over the stacks
two herons, leafless birch   But this
is a photograph from another decade   another country
What is not recorded there are danger signs, bunkers
warheads   metal beneath a compartment wavy

*   *   *

What is not recorded
might be as simple as a portrait from 1940
my grandfather in his gumboots in front of the cowshed
Perhaps he dreams there   early morning, his face
already turned to shadow   the photograph evaporating
and his heart like clockwork.   It's machinery he loves:
Give it to Mac, the neighbours say   He'll fix it.
He knows he's not much of a farmer   but hell,
he's a good Kiwi   he can fix anything,
except the farm   and his own life.   He muses there
alone at the edge of the garden with the gate
into which he has carved the name Arrochar
so that it will open out into everything:
two herons   leafless birch
a photograph his granddaughter will take in 1990

In Egypt in the Great War he found an alabaster head
in Surrey he found love   He is only forty-seven,
surely   he can still make something

★   ★   ★

Dear Mrs Macfarlane,   It is with very great sorrow
In the dry dock   the plates of the hull
In his room   a fallen beam

There is so little one can say

She turned the soil of the garden   It was almost winter

except that he died in the service of the Empire

She buried her anger deep in the ground.
She ran the farm.

CONSTANCE GERALDINE MACFARLANE 1893–1977

Her name and the dates of her life are a plain inscription on a
boulder set above the bare yellow paddock of winter grass
where she most lives, where her ashes were scattered, where for
years she'd set her jaw and grubbed the gorse in obstinate
struggle with the soil and the colonising, tenacious shrub it
harboured.

From here the house is a square tin roof nestling between the
fold of the hill and a finger of bush. We go down through the
yards at the back of the woolshed. Ramshackle fences, every-
thing at different angles, askew. The spaces of childhood
diminished   rainlashed but still magical, like a peeling sha-
dow.

I go down in fear of the Alsatians I know are there (old
childhood phobia). For strangers live here, incomers   with
city dogs. I go down knowing I carry the past, like a cup which
spills from the hand on to what is: this neglected house in
rough grass, gardenless. My grandmother's transitory flamboy-
ant art a nostalgia of fluttering colour.

All she kept buried has been set free by her death. It grows
under the house, cracks its foundations, swells and splits its grey
weatherboards, sloughs off the window sills. The house is a
family pod burst open to show the bastard inheritances of
disapproval, resentment, denial. Generations of the family idyll
that said you cannot be yourself. Disappointment, the refusal of
love.

Listen. There are other voices. Other angers lift the house.
Angers from the time of acquisition (eighty thousand acres, a
bargain at two hundred pounds). Angers from the time of
division: the arcadian dream out of the burnt ground. In the
twenties Kai Tahu from Wairewa worked as casual labour on
the Pakeha farms: it was the natural order. For was it not the
coming of the Pakeha which gave the land its value?

The gate carved in my grandfather's hand opens to childhood

journeys (the heady garden, the couched valley) and the journey we make now: the loaded southerly opening out over the flat at the head of the lake. No, not many Maori here now, my uncle says as we drive through. These days most of the houses are second homes for people from town.

The Promissory Notes

In Memoriam

Behind the gaudy face of the Early Settlers' Museum memories
and forgetfulness: a Scottish dirk; a cross of human hair given to
Annie Bathgate; a walking stick made of wood from the farm at
Mossgiel; James Hogg's desk; a programme of pipe music and
songs from a Burns Club meeting, Miss M. Ramsay singing
'My heart is Sair': a depository of discarded inheritances, of
Victorian pomposities and overwrought tableware, all the
clutter of letters and locks of hair.

Tier upon tier of faces, the frames inscribed with their names
and the names and dates of the ships they came on, towers over
the ornate furniture, the silver bric-a-brac, the bulging sofas.
They are the progenitors, the husbands and wives who came
out on the *Philip Laing*, the *John Wickliffe*, the *Phoebe Dunbar*.
Married couples named Thomson, Bissell, Nicolson, Shand.
Mrs Robert Burns née Elizabeth Campbell Douglas on the
Jura. Mrs James Wallace on the ship *Alpine*. These are the faces
of respectable Dunedin, of the Bible and the *Encyclopedia
Britannica*, of New Edinburgh and the godly experiment.

The Colony of Otago Revealed to the Elect

From the ends of the earth we gave thanks to the Lord
for the dream vouchsafed us of a Christian settlement
its streets and kirks, its places of learning
concentrated and contiguous   upright, the working model
of a market town   its inhabitants tradespeople
artisans   earning a living by honest toil

But we were hollow, restless   The life gnawed at us
North of the Waitaki the Anglicans were making money

We turned our backs on the inhuman tracts of the hills
the whisperings beyond   That way was emptiness
illusion   and no life for a pillar of the Kirk

Isolated there men lost communion with their own kind
forsook Sunday worship   became idolators of land
and money   fell under its spell in glittering waters
rivers of ice   Their eyes betrayed them
lost to the murmuring country of the imagination
her bush-choked gulches and winter passes

And the worshippers of the land rode out   and struggled
with speargrass and matagouri   and breaking through the
watershed set fire to the scrub that they might drive sheep over
the passes   And they laid claim to the living earth and
parcelled out the footsteps of those who had gone before them.

An Annotation to the Account
by Charles Kettle, Surveyor

On convulsed green I set my grid: a formal end
to the hapless filth of the old world   Dunedin
was to be a town fit for a godly experiment

The ships dropped anchor to avenues multiplied
as cleanly as equations   Princes Street was divided
by tree stumps, tussock transected my pattern of pegs
I was abused for my tardiness by folk who had no notion
of the intricacies of the surveyor's art
his tribulations in such terrain as this

I insisted on straightness but the land would not obey me
(even in my dreams it dipped   wayward and irrational)
By day it rose up   buckled against my thoroughfares
My streets hung over gulches, curved into steps   but I
pressed onward   instructed, with theodolite and wooden
    rule
to build New Edinburgh   a footprint inked indelibly
across the contours   order and rectitude

Scheelite in a bottle
from Buckleburn Creek
A ball of string, a ball
of chewed wool from a sheep's stomach
A cone in a split pine log
A pan handle, a rusty sieve
A lantern
A raw nugget
These are the entrails

A Woman Absent from the Museum
Muses on her Life in South Dunedin

Those of us whom no one thought to photograph
are here as ghosts   to give the lie
to bread without scarceness   freedom by
honest toil   our lungs choked with the motes
of our sewing, its fibres wound around our throats
and lives: a narrative of nights
without coals to keep the grate alight
of eyes sunk into pouches of skin and sleep
of fingers bound by need to the incessant needle

No new world   No paradise
a grime-smeared house where damp clung
to the weather boards   a valley where smoke hung
all year above a clanking factory
and yet we dreamt   of wonderful simplicities:
fresh vegetables in a cottage garden
a geranium on a window sill   and everything clean
We dreamt   for dreaming's free, nothing
could stop us   of what we had been promised
of what bread without scarceness might have meant

Dunedin   A Walking Narrative

I stroll through the city they made: north into the valley we lived in when I was three (sharp muzzled dogs bark at me from a fence, the valley shuts me in): south, between the lines of the survey pegs, past the Inland Revenue and the rug importers, the traffic sidling and swinging, a man in a wheelchair crossing diagonally in the mid-afternoon sunlight, down Princes Street, where the Maori sold fish and grain and potatoes to the struggling Pakeha, past Bezett's Quality Meats and the Canton Café, past the Bank of New Zealand squat-columned and grandiose, past the greening stone of a tacky Victorian cross and a hotel from which astonished gargoyles built with gold gawp at the new harshness to a desolate green where mechanics lounge in the door of a motor repairers' at smoko and a Chinese woman anxiously jiggles her baby, turning uphill for a split-second view of St Kilda before the clouds spill not rain, it takes me a moment to realise, not blossom driven in the wind, but hail, diving down the valley gutter, driving me through the Devil's Half Acre (opium dens and prostitutes calling from doorways in 1900) and back up Princes Street to the Tip Top Café where at the next table, lottery tickets spread out among the cigarette stubs and the coffee cups, a Maori family play instant Kiwi.

54

A Woman of Kai Tahu and Kati Mamoe
Addresses the Author and the Author's Tribe

Are you surprised to find us in the late twentieth century
at a café table in the centre of Dunedin
you who thought to wrap us in nostalgia
to place us in a fiction among the sandstone sinkers
and greying harpoon heads of the museum?

Were we to have become as numb as the clubs and basalt adzes
to have lain our bodies down
alongside notched bird spears   as fragile
as the bones of birds   to have become
as thin as needles   as translucent
as the slivers of greenstone   to have been broken
as utterly as the perfectly broken-shelled egg of the Moa
leaving behind us only what you needed: a mythos
for your new country   the song of its creation?

In the early days you brought a stranger's goods
of blankets and whaleboats   tobacco sickness
We offered you hospitality   wisdom   children
You brought us wheat and the magnificent tuber
We accepted them as a gift
(travelling into another tribe's territory
we ourselves would have brought such presents)
We listened to the Pakeha god and learned his trick of writing

Was this the point at which we were parted from our mother
the earth   this island?

Here are the promissory notes:
the map the surveyor Tuckett made of the Taieri plain
from the Matau to the mouth of the Harbour   (The land
you called the Otago Block   one tenth of all of which
we were to keep)   a string of blue glass beads
the colour of a Scotsman's eye and as huge as gobstoppers
and the model (a tiny seedpod of hungers)
of the ship on whose decks when you departed your country
you sang to the glory of God

HE SHALL HAVE DOMINION ALSO FROM SEA TO SEA
AND FROM THE RIVER UNTO THE ENDS OF THE EARTH
(from the Matau to the mouth of the harbour)

Was this the moment at which we were parted from our
    mother
the earth   this island?

THEY THAT DWELL IN THE WILDERNESS SHALL BOW DOWN
    BEFORE HIM

All else was to follow: language, custom   our mouths
as dumb as museum artifacts   But these are our voices
in the late twentieth century
not this voice from a Pakeha fiction   their voices
at the heart of the bloody network of our country

II

Earthworks

From 1925   A Prelude

At Coleridge power station on the balcony above the machine hall is a black and white photo of a works' outing, a picnic, in 1925. In the first row are boys in billowing caps, girls in bonnets. Next, seated, the wives in cloche hats. Behind them, a scatter of menfolk   a token of their working husbands' determining absence.

These unknown New Zealanders are our predecessors, our forerunners growing up in construction settlements across the new world hinterlands. Transitional people, families moving across country. The children rootless, unfettered. Growing up with the monoliths of grader and hill, seeing the earthworks happen, the penstock sections swung and lowered, our fathers, huge presences when we were two years old, tiny figures at work among the giants of mountain and river scarp.

The men there for the work, the women there for their menfolk. Lonely, thrown together over backfences and wash-ing lines   over the arms of their children. Or wretched with homesickness (wherever home was) weeping over a half-made gingham curtain in a makeshift box of a home   Or rejoicing in the huge country they had been pitched into   its open-ness, its freedom.

The glass of the photo reflects slices of machine hall, segments of hungry turbine and turning generator. The metal frames of the windows   x-rays of orange willow wands about to break into bud between electricity's strict mathematics.

The lake sloshes behind the people in the photograph, its meniscus laps their irises, sucking back under the calm of gelatin silver. Its placid surface swirls into a hidden outlet, like the pinpoint of an eye, is sucked under into the penstocks   a whirlpool   the plucked terror of the surge chamber   un-derground thunder.

VARYING LEVELS
CREATE HAZARDS ALONG

CHANGING SHORELINE
BEWARE SUBMERGED
FENCES   STUMPS
BOULDERS

At a Christmas picnic, a family get-together in 1971, the lake
no more than a thawed glacier, Maggie and I swam here, well
away from the current, for the challenge of it, wary of stitch, for
as long as we could in that ice water.

All these images: the machine hall, the lake, the memory I
superimpose on it, might be read in that photograph from
1925, in the eyes of the mothers under their cloche hats   -
visible for a split moment   all the hidden reefs of the
family   its changing shoreline and submerged fences   its
stumps and boulders.

Outside on the powerhouse wall are two stone tablets. The first
inscribed

> IN HONOUR OF HANS CHRISTIAN OERSTED,
> WHO DISCOVERED THE MAGNETIC EFFECT OF AN
> ELECTRIC CURRENT

and the second

> TO THE MEMORY OF MICHAEL FARADAY,
> WHO DISCOVERED THE METHOD OF
> PRODUCING ELECTRIC CURRENT BY THE ACTION
> OF MOVING MAGNETS

For God said, Let there be Light. And there was light. Though
at first people were afraid of it and wanted the old familiars of
lamp and fire. The new power was invisible and capricious.
Storms brought the lines down. Like a spirit, it came and went
as it pleased. But they got used to it. And good things followed:
electric milking machines, pumps and power saws, chicken
incubators. Over time they forgot its mystery, ceased to notice
the insubstantiality of the energy which lighted their kitchens
and heated ranges and water.

And the engineers looked upon His work and saw that it was good.

And God said to the engineers (or so they later recalled), I deliver into your hands the mountains   the plaited rivers   the many-mouthed shoreline and all those who dwell in the land.

★   ★   ★

This is a story from the twentieth century

of how Coleridge begat Waitaki
and Waitaki begat Highbank and Tekapo A
and Highbank begat Roxburgh
and Roxburgh begat Benmore

(IT TAKES BEEF TO BUILD A DAM they said
IT'S NOT JUST A MIGHTY BIG HUNK OF EARTH
BUT A TALE OF MEN AND MACHINERY
NATURE MOULDED TO THE WILL OF MAN)

And Benmore begat Aviemore
and Manapouri and Clyde

★   ★   ★

A woman drives her car across the Aviemore dam. She keeps driving, from one side to the other. From the trout race and the network of the switching station, from the lake with willows, all orange sunlight, to the drowned hollows of ovens containing burnt stones and the grilled terraces where the rock tries to fall back into the water, to be again the tumbling edge of the

63

Waitaki river.

I am split.
She is split.
They stand on two shores.

(She ran from one wall of the room to the opposite wall. She flung herself from cushion to cushion. She saw her own life divided.)

The woman gets out of her car and examines the split road surface on top of the dam, one side dark asphalt, the other concrete. Down and down, asphalt over earth, concrete over concrete. Impervious clay core and rip-rap over compacted silts, concrete over greywacke. Level over level, and all through it like an echo, a sonar blip, north-nor-west to south-sou-east the fault line lies deep in the earth like a dreaming shark.

Listen,
The land cracks and swells beneath them as they sleep.
They dream they are split in half.
That they float off to the west, to the east.
That they do not know who they are!

They won't hear the echo the land throws back, for they've wrapped it like a gift in brown paper and string, smoothed over its surface, as if one side were the same as the other, as if the fissure did not go down for hundreds of feet like the dark ragged mouth of a shark. They've shaken the phial of coloured sands and nothing has moved. They've bandaged the strains and fractures with groutwork. They've mastered the technology. The technology will heal the land.

The woman examines the road surface and then she looks at the rubble where the water of the lake laps against the dam. Imprisoned in it is the river. The ghost of the river calls and calls to the woman   remembering songs, bubbles, slushes over boulders   tumbling dances. If the river were free she would dance them again. (If the woman were free she would

64

dance.) But the river spreads out, turquoise flab behind the man-made girdle they have confined her in, and the woman gets back into her car and drives away downstream

past the drowned shingle, the flood-deposited silt, the layer of humus over hard clay and its pattern of bones and knives and broken stones.

They said it was the coming of the Pakeha which gave the land its value. (For what we cannot measure in acres of pasture, bales of wool, coinage, cannot be measured. It is without value.) They grazed their animals over the food-gathering places. They said the land lay idle. They burnt the plains, they burnt the ti trees and their delicate sugary stems. Part of the calendar was cut away.

Those who had kinship with the land, those whose ancestors had remained as pillars of rock, were driven out from the World of Light. And the sheep ate the hair of the land and the rabbits burrowed into its flesh and its body was given over to the engineers and what they saw was an emptiness. Over its tussock body the surveyors and geologists travelled, noting climatic conditions, surface configuration and the type of country. The mountains are ghosts, they said. They squinted through theodolites and scribbled in notebooks. Here be cloud. They marched over the surface mapping salt-laden winds, gales, snow storms in exposed places, mapping swamps and rock. Across it men planted transmission lines. They ran through the mist like knives. They were the linesmen and fitters, the electricians. They conducted tests and overhauls, fought storm and earthquake, for their task was the flow of power.

And the engineers looked upon their work (the hum of the

switching stations, the march of the pylons bearing power to the people, the ghost of the river thrashing her tail in the penstocks, the moment of transference from water to a secretive power that could make iron filings stand on end like the hair of a person encountering a taniwha). They looked at the fish spawning races, the eel channels, the treelined picnic grounds, the paradise for anglers and boaties, the family campsites with the million dollar view (what cannot be measured in money is without value). They looked at all this and saw that it was good and said Truly we are the children of the pioneers.

It has become a country of angle and voltage. Lines pierce the cloud. The mountains are ghosts. The pylons intersect the stony ground of the basin, steel giants who pick up their round feet and march through the almost empty land of Omarama, the World of Electric Light.

Riverline

Entering the valley of the Clutha
it seems at first to be a deep moist country
thighs not of moss but the colour of moss
and the distant tips of the blue hills
the berry juice blue a woman might
stain her breasts in some ancient ceremony
Here she comes dancing in her bracelets of electric wire
Here she comes carrying her bony schists
a desert witch bearing a great green meltwater river

OLD BONE PLATE   STUBBLE TOOTH
SHE WHO BLINDED TRAVELLERS AND WRAPPED THEM IN
    BLIZZARDS
SHE WHO FLUSHED OUT THE TAPEWORM SETTLEMENTS
TIPPED UP THE VESSEL OF FURIOUS MELTWATERS
THE SACRIFICIAL BOWL OF DROUGHT AND SUN
SHE DROVE A HARD BARGAIN
SHE GAVE NO WELCOME

★   ★   ★

I drive up into the tussock ridges
wheels swithering in first on a road
seamed with the winter's ravines
edged with witchety scrub
and bare sentinel thistles

This was my original landscape
I was a child with a billycan,
scrambling over rock
My hair has taken its colour
from these bleached winter grasses
the ochreous tussocks

the dark streaks of schist
My father and I walking out
into the inhuman country
beyond the dam

The wind drums on the car
This is no one's country
It belongs to no one human
but bone and the sawn edge of the rock

O let me crawl in to the fire of stories
of a voice other than the wind
and the populous stone hills

No water
And then I notice slush
in a ditch
A woman
and a lad on horses
two collies

Close to the grass
small dun birds
Way down,   the dam
the power station
all geometries

of chicken mesh, airy nets of cable, the intersecting steel of
pylons, fretwork holding a bank of soil. The wires sing in the
sun their malevolent burden.

THIS IS A DANGEROUS AREA. ALL
CHILDREN TO BE STRICTLY CONTROLLED.

But the cracked rock danced with us, and the parched earth
caressed our toes, and the lace of snow shining in a green river
hid under our eyelids forever.

Triangle
square

arc
polygon

Behind these twentieth-century geometries the older angles of
rock guard the river.

BECAUSE OF POWER STATION OPERATION,
THE CLUTHA RIVER CAN RISE
RAPIDLY. ALWAYS MAKE SURE YOU CAN
WITHDRAW IN SAFETY.

By the water's edge the willow sprouts its golden stems to the
tune of an interior geometry. The lost stanchions of the bailey
bridge are a vanished gateway where the bus from Roxburgh
used to cross the river, filled with the laughter of women. NO
PARKING. FALLING ROCK. In a hard light the angry spirits of the
old stone gods brood over the river flat: sheep, one white hut,
the Roxburgh East road skimming through gums. *If you're from
Roxburgh*, he said, *you must be a Hydro baby.*

In 1946 there was nothing here, they said, but rocks and
windswept hills. (Though above them on the ridge the stone
figures held sway guarding the gorge and the fanning apron of
river flat.)

There is nothing here, they say (though the figures hold sway
on the windswept crests) but rough paddocks, rabbit-eaten
bluffs, where there was once a township of rough-sawn houses,
one after the other, in treeless sections, on streets named for the
goldfields. A lawn and a few flowers struggling in the heat. A
milk bar, a butchery, a couple of grocer's, a greengrocer's, a
shoe shop, a chemist's, a hardware store. THE BIGGEST AND
MOST MODERN SETTLEMENT IN CENTRAL OTAGO. *We came
without a bean*, he said, *and now we have a three-piece suite and
a radiogram. I've bought the wife a fridge and a washing machine.* It
was the era of the family idyll, pinnies and a new kitchen of
painted cupboards. My mother lit a fire under the copper.
Making the bed in winter, her hands stiffened with cold. She

69

felt the baby kick inside her.

My father came home late and sat at his desk. *I'm busy*, he said. He put a fast film in his camera and went out to where under the floodlights, men were working in shifts on the dozers shoving 35,000 cubic yards of nothingness into the river. With it they fought to close the gap in the mighty Clutha. By dawn it foamed green and angry through the diversion cut. They had tamed the waters.

In the winter morning a driver struggled back up the hill to the huts, cradled for a moment in his hand a photograph of a smiling face lit by a tenement window or an old couple seated together under a crabbed tree in Dalmatia or Galway. Or he opened the back door of a house and spoke to his wife in their own language, hearing as music its Slav syllables. Though it was English they wanted for their children. In the mid-twentieth century it had become their future.

If you're from Roxburgh, he said, you have to write about apricots. How the women worked in the canning factory in the town, came home together on the bus, laughing. How the men tried to wash the masks of cement from their faces and their clothes seemed to stand up on their own.

How the concrete plug grew in the mouth of the gorge as if concrete were an unstoppable substance. Endowed with the magic odour of progress, all earth became it. It was the destiny of stone and sand and water. In the mid-twentieth century it had become their future.

Midway between the pole and the equator, I learned to stand upright. My father and I walked out into the inhuman country beyond the dam.

At midnight the sluice gates were closed and the lake began to fill behind their solid portcullis of steel. My mother woke to feed the new baby. Outside there was a hard winter frost and the water was rising over the ancient trails, over the huts and caves of the goldminers, over the lost pattern of Tamblyn's orchard.

The morning sun burnt off the frost with winter fire. The river was peeled back to the dam, its downstream bed exposed in runnels and pools and wells of schist. *It was like a gala day*, he said. *For miles downstream people were picnicking, parked up on the bank, panning for gold. Everyone, with saucepans, bowls, sieves, anything that came to hand, fossicking. Like Gala Day, and the sky a blue sweetie and a bit for everyone.*

Behind its girdle of concrete the river fattened. It was a celebration, AN END TO POWER HUNGER, electricity whenever you wanted it. POWER FOR THE SOUTH.

The water found its level and the lake shimmered in its long slit of rock which had once been a gorge. Power flowed into the grid and the river flowed again over the schist hollows and water-washed boulders. No one had found much gold but who cared; it had been such a celebration under the blue winter sky, and everyone rich with the power to come. We were the people of the new world looking to the future.

Maggie was weighed each week by the Plunket Nurse, and learned the beatific smile of the photographs. It was mid-1956 in Godzone and OUR FUTURE WAS WITH ELECTRICITY, THE CHEAPEST POWER IN THE WORLD.

ONCE AGAIN
WE BRING YOU
NEW LOW PRICES AND
SENSATIONAL NEW FEATURES
OVER TEN DIFFERENT MODEL
KELVINATOR REFRIGERATORS
SIDE-MOUNTED FREEZER with 2 ice trays
deep meat tray   full width crisper
WHITEWAY KING OF ELECTRIC DISHWASHERS
(Yours for only £89)
BENDIX AUTOMATIC WASHER
(£119 cash price or 23/3 weekly)
AUTOMATIC NECCHI-SUPERNOVA
(Over 200,000 stitches at your fingertips)

But this might have been the story
of a woman's hand burnt to a pail in winter
a rag of skin on the metal handle

of how she came to hate
the monotony of the landscape
its scorched summers and bitter winters
which meant the death of children
and the dessication of beasts

How the sun wrapped her head in madness
and the stone menagerie began to speak
telling her how everything must be eroded
must lay its bones out like the skeleton of a sheep

How she was hollow and the wind shaped her
(delicate wool still curling over neat hooves)
and the voices entered her head
(horns like pumice)
How in the end she became one with the land

I sing a woman in a kitchen at evening
making the windows glow with the strange
interior cadences of the electric hob

I sing the pure energy of the pylons
the liquid crystal surging in the pipes
I sing the vivid paddocks
the organo-phosphates   the toxic run-off

I sing the body damaged   opened
to the resonances of an infinitesimal particle
I sing the cancer

Nightfall   her mind (a great river)
dipping into sleep   (a continuum of waves)

I sing her   jolted out of sleep, waveform
disrupted: a violent landscape
I sing the seizure

I sing the volcanic
topography of the electroencephalogram
the delicate trace of the cortex

I sing   the body electric

Counterpoints

He preaches as they pass (Jesus will save them) but they turn away, seeing themselves dissolve in the windows (He will heal them) among pots of indigo and scented oils (He is their salvation). Among pouches of velvet with metal jaws, among high fast heels: here's how (they are absolved) they walk out, spring coming. Or sheathed in waterfall silk, their faces shining given back to them in ticking, jewelled faces of African gold. And above them all the global signs WELCOME TO AUCKLAND. Each building a trumpet blast to THE CAPITAL OF THE SOUTH PACIFIC, a jigsaw puzzle of past and future; the Victorians' ponderous curlicues impaled on the geometry of illusion.

The faces of the young distorted in windows, in ranked shields. The visors of riot police reflecting glass, high-flying cloud. And under the visors the unreflective faces, the drawn-down mouths, the puritanical armies of Godzone. SCHOOL'S OUT. December 1984.

Faces, bodies jostling under the banners. UNEMPLOYED WORK-ERS' ASSOCIATION, P & T ASSOCIATION, UNEMPLOYED WORK-ERS' MOVEMENT. April 1932. *A man will succeed here if he has probity and application.* The women sang 'the Red Flag'. *A man has no need of association in this country of natural abundance.* The reflections shattered became splinters, jagged bracelets of glass through which to grab for cigarettes, whisky, diamonds, fallen gold. A man lined his pockets with ticking clocks, youths in dress jackets strutted on a dangerous catwalk, the police surged down Queen Street in a brutal wave.

At Tennyson Street Mrs Graham had come hammering on the kitchen door to Alice and the boys, telling the news from the wireless. Riot, its flames like wildfire. And the Union meeting in the town hall, Charlie'd be stuck in there.

Charlie Fellows, my grandfather, was a telegraph linesman, a trade union activist. His father and grandfather were master bricklayers; big-chinned, stocky, handsome people with careful hands. His grandfather had come out to New Zealand in the

77

1880s. *For here a man must be the architect of his own fortunes.* He bought a section in Onehunga and the family lived under a tarpaulin there while they built a brick house for themselves. There was work for builders. Auckland was spreading out over the Maori farms, over the peach groves and fields of maize.

For the Lord thy God bringeth thee into a good land, a land of brooks of water, of fountains and depths that spring out of valleys and hills; A land of wheat, and barley, and vines, and fig trees, and pomegranates; a land of oil, olive and honey; A land wherein thou shalt eat bread without scarceness, thou shalt not lack any thing in it.

I'm standing in the museum gazing at a grainy black and white photograph of a Maori family lined up in shapeless European clothes in front of a ramshackle whare. Loss is written across their faces, into their hands, into the grey seams of their garments. It is 1928 and they are lined up to be shot by a white photographer as a record of a dying race.

In 1928 my father was seven years old doing sums at a desk in a school in Northcote built by his grandfather. Across the water in Manukau a child was being beaten for speaking her own language. And deep in the volcanic heart of the island a man was carving a door lintel out of the living wood of his people.

In that same year in front of the house in Onehunga, the Fellows family lined up together for the camera. They all beam happily out at the photographer. There's Grandfather Fellows with the bushy moustache, and Ernie, he was a master bricklayer too, and Eric, and Eileen, Jean's mother, who married George Sweet, and Auntie Dot, huge woman, and Esma, who married John Thomson and had seventeen kids, and Leslie, the youngest of the brothers. It's a celebration, Christmas, a wedding maybe. They smile for the camera, the women shading their eyes with their hats, the men a little too warm in their best suits but content, with the holiday, with their country, with the language in which they tell jokes to one another and stories to the children.

Family photographs: the brothers as young men, jaunty-chinned; Charlie with Alice Fitzgerald on their wedding day in 1919; Alice in 1926 with my father and uncle on the Sydney harbour ferry on her first visit back.

In 1917 when my grandmother crossed the Tasman loss was a secret coin she had carried with her, something durable, shining, lucky. Only years later her sons would say, I think there was someone, in Sydney, before the war. Her sisters, Dear Flo, Ada, Berthe, Maggie, she consigned to letters. She put her family at a distance, that was the story. She turned her face to the new life, got a job at the City Treasury, married a man faithful to principles and people, younger than she was, proud of her. Is that the story? In Northcote during the pinched years of the thirties she bought the stock for the co-operative and did the books. When Charlie retired they bought a shop. GIs flocked in to buy newspapers and maga-zines. She was a clever woman. My mother would say, bossy like her eldest son. And why did she marry a man so much younger than she was? Charlie was such a darling.

Northcote now is a place you pass. The motorway straddles Tennyson Street, Sulphur Beach, my father's childhood. The bus skims by on its way north. Auckland unwalkable: long straps of flyovers, sheets of water. The present swallows us.

By the time we knew her, ageing, irascible, not given to cuddles, she was Granny Fellows, a black-dressed territorial woman with wasp stings at her kitchen door. She and my uncle had moved south by then to a house under the cone of Mangere pa. Salt spray burnt the vegetables in the market gardens and blasted the edge of the kumara pits high on the crater of Mangere hill, but on the kitchen wall Loo's calendar bloomed with flowers and fruit, the sun shone and we drove out to Auntie Tillie in Waiuku.

This land and harbour of Manukau   is a ring of sacred places.
This land and harbour of Manukau   is a ring of despoilations.

*From Mangere to the Waikato River: 58,475 hectares of confiscated
    land.*

*The mudflats taken for the airport, the sewage treatment plant,
the LPG wharf terminal.*

The shellfisheries unpredictable, dwindling, despoiled.

The body of water enriched, sickened, polluted.

The oyster shells empty
but the fishshop window glittering with oysters.

*Manukau was their garden of the sea,
life-sustaining body of water*

enriched, sickened, polluted.

We drive south around the rim of the Manukau, Donna at the
wheel talking of other places – her father's people from Lewis,
the snapshots from Carloway filled with ageing faces.

That's where Eric and Tillie's farm was, my uncle points out a
gulch of tumbled pasture, a shed about to topple. During the
depression when the Post Office was cutting wages Eric got out
and went farming. The Thomsons farmed here too. That was

80

their place up the hill, better land, not as heavy as the flat.

(Ah, my father remembers, the summers at Maioro, the marram grass, the sand hills, the long luminous trek to the sea.)

From Mangere to the Waikato River 58,475 hectares of confiscated land.

In the thirties there was a relief camp opposite Eric's farm, government work for the unemployed planting trees to stablise the dunes.

1,490 hectares compulsorily purchased from the Waikato tribes for the planting of the Waiuku State Forest.

Conifers on the skyline, pyramids of black sand.

Maioro, the ancient burying ground desecrated, mined for ironsands.

DANGER   KEEP OUT

The burying ground once ringed with ancestors,
their dangerous and sacred faces of carved wood.

DANGER   KEEP OUT

HIGH PRESSURE SLURRY PIPELINE

THE WORLD'S FIRST POLYURETHANE-LINED HIGH PRESSURE UNDERGROUND PIPELINE TRANSPORTING ABRASIVE GRANULAR MATERIALS BY POSITIVE DISPLACEMENT PUMPS.

(Ah the marram grass, the sand hills of Maioro, the long luminous trek to the sea.)

The slurry pipeline crosses the land from Maioro to Glenbrook, from the Waikato River to the Manukau harbour carrying ironsands to Glenbrook steel mill, the used water disposed of into the harbour. The waters of the Waikato mixed with the waters of the Manukau, the spirits of the waters mixed

81

together.

The judge ruled that the Planning Tribunal was required to apply RATIONAL, SCIENTIFIC AND MANAGERIAL TECHNIQUES IN THE MANAGEMENT OF THE NATURAL ENVIRONMENT, THAT PURELY METAPHYSICAL CONCERNS COULD NOT BE TAKEN INTO ACCOUNT.

Heading for Pollok, we pass a Maori woman stooped at the roadside gathering puha among the grass and brambles.

I don't know what you expect to find, my uncle's saying. There's not much there. A few cottages, a school, a weatherboard church newly painted as brazenly white as fine weather cumulus, someone mowing a lawn, sunshine like honey.

Imagine you are standing with your back to sombre paintings in gilded frames. From the window, smirr drifts across ruffled branches. You descend the steps of the garden, yourself a point in its perspective. Across the river voices like mist rise from the reeds. The heritor, desiring a pastoral vista, cleared the old township and laid it out to fields. For Pollok is a memory and a dispossession though this is not entered, merely: *Pollok. Auckland Province. Locality Franklin County. Farming. 15 miles northwest by road from Waiuku. Named by pioneer settlers from Pollokshaws, a suburb of Glasgow.*

Beside the road a Waikato woman stoops to gather puha from among the grass and brambles.

For Pollok is a memory and a dispossession, though this is not entered.

From a finger of land running northwards to the mouth of the harbour we head downhill. The old wharf, long disused, is a jumble of collapsed slabs slippy with algae. The Manukau stinks at our feet. Across the arm of water the stacks of the steel mill throw up plumes of smoke.

82

THE PRODUCTION OF STEEL FROM TITANOMAGNETITE SAND IS A
WORLD FIRST, AND THIS PLANT AT GLENBROOK, SOUTH AUCK-
LAND, IS THE ONLY ONE OF ITS TYPE. IT WAS DESIGNED TO USE A
PROCESS LARGELY DEVELOPED BY NEW ZEALAND ENGINEERS TO
PRODUCE STEEL FROM INDIGENOUS IRONSAND AND SUB-BITU-
MINOUS COAL – THE BIGGEST SINGLE-SITE DEVELOPMENT IN
NEW ZEALAND.

Positive displacement, they believed, was a good thing for the
country.

Dissolving Song

I

On the television screen a woman
spins the wheel of fortune: his ancestor was

a border reiver   She spins the wheel:

his ancestor was   the winner   was
a border reiver   wins a gold chain   a dishwasher
all their treasures   a holiday in Rarotonga   dollars
and Estates   Forests and Fisheries   a Toyota Starlet

II

All their treasures

are winners: the flat nameless tiki
dollar after dollar   (never touched by the oil of the body)
Paua shell cave after cave   generations become
brooch   earring   row of shell and stone
Pounamu who was once a fish
and Tiki's paua-inlaid tongue potent from totara
among sheepskin bloodjacket & kiwi paperweight
and a bird creature lifting its wings
over the outlines of
ROCK ART NEW ZEALAND

I saunter in   I am incognito
I am an English tourist
among tourists buying
leather   and the luxury fuzz of
handknitted merino wool from Central Otago
(Ah my heart land   of cloud pearl, tussock needle)
Black teeshirt screen-printed to stiff gold:
MAORI ROCK ART NEW ZEALAND outlined
over replicating loops netted to cloth
by sweated labour in the Philippines

But the bird creature made of the shapes of the moon
the cusp-shaped elements   raises its wings

over the limestone entrails of my island inland
over its paddocks (I could have loved)
over its magnetic fields (High Voltage Direct Current)

What I have

what I have   remember:

III

How in the beginning it was winter.
Now spring sails over the Waitemata
on my last day in the country of my childhood
(Is it that country?)

This evening we'll head over to Manurewa
to my father's cousin just home from Europe
(from Don's family in Lewis (lost and found)
from Leslie in London, my father in Yorkshire)
She gives me a photograph to take back
of the two of them on Ashness bridge (See that's Jean
Eileen and George Sweet's daughter   And that's Al
Charlie's eldest, who married Geraldine Macfarlane)
Twenty years since we last did this:
A tradition I tell her

But before then I will already have packed my clothes
the rolls of colour film   my notebook
(the books gone last week   two boxes, surface)
I will have packed the earrings the apple the bowl
the spoons the found shells   I will have packed
the wave-eaten ring in which a gastropod
once encoded its miraculous spiral
And it will sing there in my luggage
as it will sing in the hold of the 747
as it lifts with me into the southern hemisphere midnight
as it sings to me now

spiralling between something and nothing
simply found   meaningful

The Night Maps

Farewell
the plane lifts
We are a small independent nation
(the bird creature raises its wings)
the multiple lights of the airfield fall away
into midnight beside the Manukau
We are aswim on the southern surface of the globe
Auckland ablaze and still talking to itself
on Bell Atlantic and Ameritech
The Capital of the South Pacific
its global signs
KPMG Peat Marwick   Minolta   IBM

diminish beyond us   eating
into the dark star of the pumicelands
woodpulp stacked on the wharves
and wrapped in night along the fronds of coast
the black stain of the Tarawera
its bouquet of foaming ponds
by Fletcher Challenge
and the lifeline of a river
brought to you from the nub of an island
steel hearts pumping it into power
into Auckland ablaze and carrying a torch
for Aiwa   BP   Citibank
Farewell
We raise a jug
to Mobil   Price Waterhouse   Elders IXL
We are a small independent nation

The plane slides into thinning troposphere
South of us a woman twists on her bed
and the ponies snort in the paddock
The country dreams in the backbeat of the dams
and a bird creature raises its wings over
the tumble of a harbour   the buried cables
of the Cook Strait Link
the cropped vineyards

the Mount Hutt ski field
picture-postcard alps blanked out by night
the plains where Fran sleeps dreaming of grandmotherhood
towards the blood of Aramoana
the smokescreen of the Alcan smelter.
The spun melody of the powerlines
30,000 gigawatt hours per annum
cradles the sleepers
stirs the small furred animals, the heavy cattle
and at the margin of a stand of bush
a morepork   bright eye alert in leafcurl

This is Farewell

Now you will enter
the night maps   the unknown
formations of crystal

Over the Pacific the constellations will rise
a solemn mirror
to the ocean's hidden phosphorescence
fire-encrusted   slip

over the equator in their Greek names
towards the daylit miles of tundra
and magnetic north

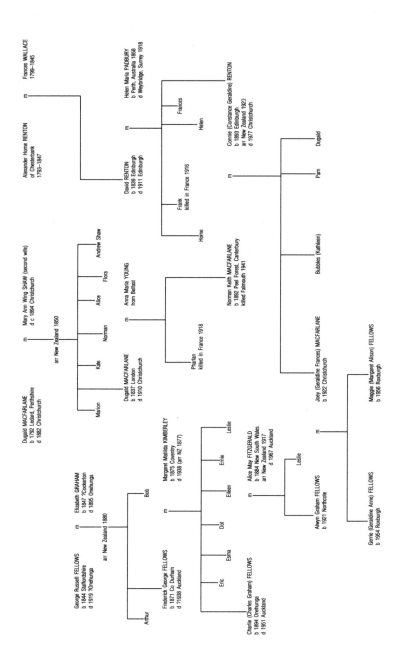

Dugald MACFARLANE
b 1792 Ledard, Perthshire
d 1882 Christchurch

m

Mary Ann Wing SHAW (second wife)
d c 1894 Christchurch

arr New Zealand 1850

Frances WALLACE
1799–1845

m

Alexander Home RENTON
of Chesterbank
1793–1847

Helen Maria PADBURY
b Perth, Australia 1858
d Weybridge, Surrey 1918

David RENTON
b 1839 Edinburgh
d 1911 Edinburgh

m

Marion

Kate

Norman

Alice

Flora

Andrew Shaw

Frances

Helen

Connie (Constance Geraldine) RENTON
b 1893 Edinburgh
arr New Zealand 1920
d 1977 Christchurch

Dugald MACFARLANE
b 1837 London
d 1910 Christchurch

m

Anna Maria YOUNG
from Belfast

Pharlan
killed in France 1918

Norman Keith MACFARLANE
b 1892 Peel Forest, Canterbury
killed Falmouth 1941

Frank
killed in France 1916

Home

Pam

Dugald

George Russell FELLOWS
b 1844 Staffordshire
d 1919 ?Onehunga

m

Elizabeth GRAHAM
b 1847 ?Cockerton
d 1895 Onehunga

arr New Zealand 1880

Arthur

Bob

Frederick George FELLOWS
b 1871 Co Durham
d ?1938 Auckland

m

Margaret Matilda KIMBERLEY
b 1875 Coventry
d 1938 (arr NZ 1877)

Eric

Esma

Dot

Eileen

Ernie

Leslie

Bubbles (Kathleen)

Joey (Geraldine Frances) MACFARLANE
b 1922 Christchurch

Charlie (Charles Graham) FELLOWS
b 1894 Onehunga
d 1961 Auckland

Alice May FITZGERALD
b 1884 New South Wales
arr New Zealand 1917
d 1967 Auckland

m

Leslie

Alwyn Graham FELLOWS
b 1921 Northcote

m

Gerrie (Geraldine Anne) FELLOWS
b 1954 Roxburgh

Maggie (Margaret Allison) FELLOWS
b 1956 Roxburgh

Notes

Epigraph

'The tests I need to pass are prescribed by the spirits of place   who understand travel but not amnesia' comes from 'The Spirit of Place' by Adrienne Rich in *A Wild Patience has Taken Me This Far: Poems 1978–1981* (New York: W. W. Norton, 1981).

A Chronicle of Beginnings

I

The Lord be praised, only infants have been taken. These lines were suggested by an account of the voyage of the *Sir George Seymour* in *From The Star: Early Shipping Days* (newspaper clippings in the Turnbull Library, Wellington).

II

Ranginui   Papatuanuku   and between them Tane Mahuta. In Maori creation myth light came into the world through the separation of the original parents, Rangi the Sky Father and Papa the Earth Mother. Of all their children, it was Tane Mahuta, the god of trees, who was able to push his parents apart.

Maui was the demi-god and prankster of Maori myth who brought both fire and death into the world. His grandmother's jawbone was the archetypal bone tool with which he clubbed the sun and fished up New Zealand's North Island.

III

Kumara: the small sweet potato of Polynesia.

IV

a hilly surface cloathed with Verdure; dayly we saw smookes; the sandbanks well store'd with Cockles, and clams and in many places were Rock Oysters; soil rich and proper for cultivation; a brave, open, warlike people; Two large Islands divided by a strait or passage of 4 or 5 Leagues broad. These lines are quoted from *The Journals of Captain James Cook, Vol. I: the Voyage of the Endeavour 1768–1771* edited by J. C. Beaglehole (Cambridge: Published for The Hakluyt Society by the University Press, 1955, 2nd edition 1968).

93

V
Welcome to New Zealand. The New Zealand Customs and Agricultural Quarantine Declaration.

Bloodlines
Canterbury Museum Negative No. 1285: Dugald Macfarlane
Pukeko: a New Zealand swamp hen.

Young Dugald with Dreamscape
A feel for the life of the early European pastoralists came from Samuel Butler's *A First Year in Canterbury Settlement* edited by A. C. Brassington and P. B. Maling (Blackwood & Janet Paul, Auckland & Hamilton, 1964. First published Longman, Green, Longman, Roberts, & Green, 1863). Information about Albury Station came from Robert Pinney's *Early South Canterbury Runs*.

Kate's Song
Idiot child. Lady Charlotte Godley in *Letters from Early New Zealand* describes two of the Macfarlane children as 'idiots'. The remark was cut from some editions of the book.

Ghost Page for Mary Ann at Racecourse Hill
Ledard was sold in 1860 and became part of the neighbouring station, Racecourse Hill. Details can be found in L. G. D. Acland, *The Early Canterbury Runs* (Christchurch: Whitcomb & Tombs Ltd, revised edition, 1946).

Narrative Subjects
Local history of the Berwickshire parishes of Eyemouth and Coldingham came from the three Statistical Accounts of Scotland. The never fully anonymous heritor of the first poem might even be John Renton, Esq. of Chesterbank, the compiler (in lieu of an encumbent minister) of the report on the Parish of Coldingham in the Statistical Account of the 1790s. The lively Eyemouth Museum gave me both a sense of the locality's past and the location of the Rentons' townhouse, the walled garden of which appears in several of the poems.

The Notation of a Dream Recounted
by Connie Renton to her Granddaughters
The Eyemouth Disaster took place on 14 October 1881, twelve years before my grandmother was born. The Hurkurs are the rocks at the harbour entrance on which some of the ships foundered.

Tableau
Kai Tahu (or Ngai Tahu) is the predominant South Island tribe.

Pakeha: white-skinned strangers. The word is now used to denote New Zealanders of European, especially British, descent.

The Promissory Notes
The Colony of Otago Revealed to the Elect
But we were hollow, restless. A sense of the inwardness and stagnation of early Dunedin can be found in a letter from Charles Edward Douglas in John Pascoe's *Mr Explorer Douglas* (Wellington: A. H. & A. W. Reed, 1957).

An Annotation to the Account   by Charles Kettle, Surveyor
For the description of Dunedin when the first settlers arrived I am indebted to Erik Olssen, *A History of Otago* (Dunedin: John McIndoe, 1984).

Dunedin   A Walking Narrative
Smoko: teabreak.

The Devil's Half Acre was a phrase used in 1906 by the *Otago Daily Times* and quoted in R. J. Johnson (ed.), *Urbanisation in New Zealand: Geographical Essays* (Wellington: A. H. & A. W. Reed, 1973).

A Woman of Kai Tahu and Kati Mamoe
Addresses the Author and the Author's Tribe
Kati Mamoe were the dominant tribe in the South Island before Kai Tahu. Most South Island Maori trace descent from both tribes.

95

The Matau is the Maori name of the river Cook called the Molyneux and which, after the Scottish settlement, became known as the Clutha.

Earthworks
From 1925   A Prelude
IT TAKES BEEF TO BUILD A DAM. The opening of Benmore power station in 1965 was marked by a celebratory issue of the *Otematata Chronicle* filled with wonderfully self-congratulatory advertisements for everything from meat to concrete pipe.

Taniwha: a water spirit or monster.

The placename Omarama is a corruption of Te ao marama meaning the World of Light; the world created by the separation of the bodies of Rangi and Papa.

Riverline
If you're from Roxburgh, he said, *you must be a Hydro baby*. From a conversation with Phil Turnock.

We came without a bean, and now we have a three-piece suite and a radiogram. For the account of Roxburgh Hydro township I am indebted to W. J. Campbell's *Hydrotown* (Dunedin: mimeographed thesis, University of Otago, 1957).

It was like Gala Day. My description of the damfill is based on conversations with my father, Al Fellows.

Godzone: a contraction of God's Own Country. The phrase is redolent of a certain period of New Zealand history.

ELECTRICITY, THE CHEAPEST POWER IN THE WORLD. The *Roxburgh Souvenir Supplement* of the *Evening Star*, 24 July 1956, with its advertisements for a multiplicity of electrical goods, gives a wonderful sense of the new era and its language. Its editorial on the diversion of the Clutha River and the building of the dam catches the excitement.

I sing   the body electric. A reference to the Walt Whitman poem 'I sing the Body Electric', in *Leaves of Grass* (New York: The New American Library, Inc, 1958).

Counterpoints

My description of the 1932 Auckland riot draws on family reminiscence and on the account in the *New Zealand Herald*, 15 April 1932, quoted in *NZ Herald: 100 Years of News: Centennial Record 1863–1963*.

Miles Fairburn's *The Ideal Society and its Enemies: The Foundations of Modern New Zealand Society 1850–1900* (Auckland University Press, 1989, reprinted 1990) is particularly interesting on the ideas of utopia and natural abundance which informed the colonisation of New Zealand. Several lines in this sequence were drawn from eulogies to New Zealand life quoted by Fairburn; James Buller's *New Zealand: Past and Present* (London: 1880) and W. D. Hay's *Brighter Britain or Settler and Maori in Northern New Zealand* (2 vols, London: 1880).

Pa: a fortified village. The pa at Mangere is built on one of Auckland's ancient volcanoes.

From Mangere to the Waikato River. Much of the information in this sequence was drawn from Ranginui Walker's history *Ka Wha Whai Tonu: Struggle Without End* (Auckland: Penguin Books (NZ) Ltd, 1990). See Chapter 12 'Ma te Ture te Ture e Patu: Only the Law can Defeat the Law' for his discussion of the Manukau claim to the Waitangi Tribunal.

Information on the Glenbrook steel mill and slurry pipeline came from *Engineering to 1990*, edited for IPENZ (The Institution of Professional Engineers New Zealand Incorporated) by F. N. Stace (Wellington: Engineering Publications Co. Ltd, 1990).

RATIONAL, SCIENTIFIC AND MANAGERIAL TECHNIQUES . . .
Judge Turner's ruling for New Zealand Steel in the appeal by Nganeko Minhinnick for the Tainui tribes against the

granting of a water right, quoted in Walker, *Ka Wha Whai Tonu.*

Puha: an edible plant, sow thistle.

The description of Pollok came from E. S. Dollimore's *The New Zealand Guide* (Wise's Directories, 1962).

Dissolving Song
All their treasures . . . Estates   Forests and Fisheries: references to the Maori and English texts of the 1840 Treaty of Waitangi, the English text of which guaranteed 'to the Chiefs and Tribes of New Zealand and to the respective families and individuals thereof the full exclusive and undisturbed possession of their Lands and Estates Forests Fisheries and other properties'. See I. H. Kawharu (ed.), *Waitangi: Maori & Pakeha Perspectives of the Treaty of Waitangi* (Auckland: Oxford University Press, 1989).

The Night Maps
Aramoana is the small South Island township where in 1990 a young man shot dead thirteen people before being shot dead himself by police.